What about me, what do I want?

Becoming Assertive

by Barbara Small, M.A.

Note for Librarians: A cataloguing record for this book is available from Library and Archives Canada at www.collectionscanada.ca/amicus/index-e.html

ISBN 1-4120-6931-9

Printed in Victoria, BC, Canada. Printed on paper with minimum 30% recycled fibre. Trafford's print shop runs on "green energy" from solar, wind and other environmentally-friendly power sources.

TRAFFORD
PUBLISHING™

Offices in Canada, USA, Ireland and UK

This book was published *on-demand* in cooperation with Trafford Publishing. On-demand publishing is a unique process and service of making a book available for retail sale to the public taking advantage of on-demand manufacturing and Internet marketing. On-demand publishing includes promotions, retail sales, manufacturing, order fulfilment, accounting and collecting royalties on behalf of the author.

Book sales for North America and international:
Trafford Publishing, 6E–2333 Government St.,
Victoria, BC V8T 4P4 CANADA
phone 250 383 6864 (toll-free 1 888 232 4444)
fax 250 383 6804; email to orders@trafford.com

Book sales in Europe:
Trafford Publishing (UK) Limited, 9 Park End Street, 2nd Floor
Oxford, UK OX1 1HH UNITED KINGDOM
phone 44 (0)1865 722 113 (local rate 0845 230 9601)
facsimile 44 (0)1865 722 868; info.uk@trafford.com

Order online at:
trafford.com/05-1842

10 9 8 7 6 5 4 3 2 1

Table of Contents

Introduction.. 1

What is Assertiveness?...............................7

The 4 communication styles 7
Testing your communication IQ................... 17
Beginning your journey to becoming assertive......... 23

What Keep You Non-Assertive? 27

How did you learn to be non-assertive? 27
How do you keep yourself non-assertive today?...... 28
What prevents you from being assertive?................. 31
Self-esteem and assertiveness.. 32

What Do You Believe About Being
Assertive? 33

What are your beliefs that keep you non-assertive?. 33
Self-talk 35
The world does not revolve around you 40
Are you afraid of appearing selfish?........................... 42
A bill of assertive rights 43

What are Your Obstacles to Becoming
Assertive? 47

Feelings, they're nothing more than feelings 47
What's the worse thing that could happen?.............. 51
Yes, and then what? 52
Whose problem is it anyway?.................................... 53
Being assertive is a choice... 57
If not now, when? 58

That's their choice..58
Making excuses 59

What Else Do I Need to Know About Becoming Assertive?.......................... 63

Assertiveness can be people-specific and/or situation-specific. 63
Assertion self-assessment table 65
What about me, what do I want? 69
Ideas to keep in mind 73

How Do I Become Assertive?...................... 75

How assertive are you already?...............................75
Tips to expressing yourself assertively......................77
The beginnings of assertive communication 78
Sample assertive responses.....................................80
Tips for dealing with challenging situations.............82
    Saying "no"..*82*
    Setting boundaries...*86*
    Accepting compliments......................................*88*
    Avoid playing the victim...................................*89*
    That is not about me........................................*90*
    Don't try to argue someone out of his/her opinion............*91*
    Avoid trying to be a mind-reader.......................*92*
    Dealing with criticism......................................*93*
    Perhaps. *94*
    Avoid keeping score..*95*
    The blame game...*97*
    That's not my problem......................................*97*
    If you could do it differently. *100*

What Do I Need to Remember? 101

Introduction

I haven't always been assertive. Actually several months ago I suddenly realized how assertive I had become. I finally noticed it. And it felt good. I felt more confident and calmer. I was happy to realize that I stand up for myself and express my opinion more now that I ever did in the past. I worry less about what other people think of me. I worry less about whether the people closest to me are happy with the choices that I make. In the past, I would even have worried about what strangers thought about my choices.

I no longer need to consciously make an effort to ask myself – ***"What about me, what do I want?"*** It comes naturally to me now. Repeatedly others in my life ask me to help them with their communication. Both clients and friends tell me they ask themselves, "What would Barb say about this?" Communicating assertively has become a natural part of who I am and I believe the same can happen for you.

As I said I haven't always been assertive. I spent most of my life being passive and self-conscious. I tried passive-aggressive for a while but the others in my life didn't cooperate so that didn't work very well. I grew up in a household where passive-aggressive and passive behaviour was more often the norm. I learned to be passive and focused on trying to fix things and make everything better. I learned that it was better to agree with the other person than to have a differing opinion. I also learned to swallow my feelings and needs rather than ask for them to be met.

I became a compulsive overeater for 20 years because it helped me to stuff my feelings and ignore my self. In my adolescence and early adulthood I tried being passive-aggressive. Pouting, sarcasm and feeling sorry for myself were my tools of choice. It worked with some people, but then I ended up with friends who called me on it. They said, "Yes, we know you're pouting and we're not coming to make it better. If you have something to talk to us about, you need to come to us directly".

I still went into the other room and pouted even though I told myself that they were not coming to see what was wrong. I eventually realized that it was easier to pretend that they hadn't noticed that I was upset than take the risk to approach them and directly ask for what I needed. If I did this I would have to take the risk that they might say "No", which I would have taken as a personal rejection.

Over the years I tried off and on to be assertive and very slowly it became more familiar and less scary. Of course there are times when I return back to what was familiar for most of my life. I have a habit of being controlling especially when I am stressed. When I am trying to resist something, I become directive in telling other people what to do. But in general I am assertive most of the time.

Communicating assertively can be beneficial in both our work and personal lives. Assertiveness can also be key in overcoming many issues, including addictions and other compulsive behaviours. Being assertive can help you feel more confident and meet your goals and dreams. It is a beneficial skill whether you currently tend to be passive, passive-aggressive or aggressive. In fact I often hear from people, "Gee, I'm too assertive. I don't need your class." To which I respond, "You can't be too assertive. You may be aggressive instead, so the course might be just what you need."

My wish is that you feel more confident, that you value and trust yourself more and begin to communicate assertively. I know from my personal experience and from working with clients for over a decade that it is possible to make these changes. It can be challenging at times, but the outcome is well worth the effort. Through this book I hope to help facilitate your journey by sharing what has worked for me and many others.

In the first chapter, I focus on the difference between the four styles of communication – passive, aggressive, passive-aggressive and assertive. I look at the impact of these four different styles on our relationships and provide examples to illustrate how they compare. Finally, I discuss what assertive communication looks and sounds like.

In the second chapter, you will explore how you learned to be non-assertive in the first place and how you keep yourself non-assertive now. Our belief systems play a significant role in whether or not we are assertive and in Chapter 3 we explore the impact of our beliefs and the role our negative self-talk takes in maintaining these beliefs.

For most of you this is not the first time you have tried to become more assertive. In Chapter 4, I list some of the common obstacles to becoming assertive and offer a perspective on them that will hopefully allow you to release them. Chapter 5 explores key concepts related to assertiveness that I think are important for you to know to facilitate your journey. Before you can be assertive you need to know what you want to communicate and that is where the question, **"What about me, what do I want?"** becomes an essential first step to becoming assertive.

In Chapter 6 I provide you with tips to being assertive and techniques to help you respond in specific challenging situations. I also include examples of assertive language for you to use until this way of communicating become more familiar. I know in the beginning it can feel overwhelming and feel like you are speaking a foreign language. The final chapter summarizes the key points discussed in the book.

Throughout this book I provide activities and self-reflection questions to help you to explore how the information provided applies to your own life and to help you to identify what steps you personally need to take to become more assertive.

I welcome your feedback on the information contained in this book and I would love to hear about your personal experience with becoming assertive.

Good luck and enjoy yourself.

Barb

barbsmall@shaw.ca
www.barbsmallcounselling-coaching.com

1

What is assertiveness?

To be assertive is to express your rights, to stand up for yourself, your values and your beliefs. It is to be able to express your true self - your feelings, your needs, your wants, your thoughts, and your opinions. Assertiveness skills allow you to express your rights while respecting the rights of others. In order to be assertive, we want to identify our rights, specify our needs and communicate effectively.

The 4 communication styles

Individuals' behaviours can be divided into four categories – assertive, passive, aggressive and passive aggressive. Living an *assertive* life means taking an active and responsible approach to others and to your life. Individuals who interact *passively* seldom feel happy and often put themselves down. *Aggressive* people feel in control, but they will be watching in case someone tries to beat them. They often are defensive and seldom have many friends. *Passive-aggressive* people are manipulative and controlling similar to an aggressive person, but they do so in a more passive and subtle way. A more detailed description of each of the four styles is listed on the following pages.

The 4 communication styles occur on a continuum

I have noticed after many years of counselling clients that when behaviours occur on a continuum and a person starts at one end and tries to move toward the middle, they usually move to the opposite end first. After that it becomes really difficult to move back toward the middle because it feels like you will get sucked back to where you started. The old behaviour is still familiar and the new behaviour is uncomfortable. For example, if you have been passive in the past, when you want to change you will likely find yourself moving toward the aggressive end. This occurs because we think that to make this change we must move as far from the old behaviours as possible.

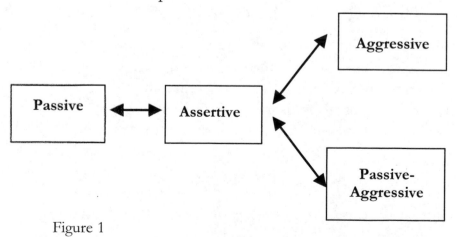

Figure 1

A Passive person tends to:

- Be quiet and timid, silent due to fear
- Avoid conflict, be a people-pleaser
- Not make eye contact
- Be a chameleon, change to suit the situation
- Not offer own opinion or express feelings
- Feel insecure, have low self-esteem
- "You're ok, I'm not ok""
- The other person's needs generally get met, yet the passive person's need to avoid conflict is met.

An Aggressive person can be:

- Loud and in your face, blunt, tactless
- Believe in "My way or the highway"
- Blaming and shaming
- Can be violent, though not necessarily so
- Sarcastic, uses jokes in a cruel way
- Controlling and manipulative
- Angry, jealous
- Takes care of self and own rights only
- Though may appear overly confident, has low self-esteem
- "I'm ok, you're not ok"
- The aggressive person's needs tend to get met over the other person's needs

A Passive-aggressive person may:

- Use silence to manipulate
- Use guilt trips and sarcasm
- Pout and play the martyr
- Excel at playing "the victim"
- Give mixed messages
- Use triangling, i.e. complains about your sister to you, but does not talk to your sister directly.
- Be controlling and manipulative
- Hint and expect mind-reading from others
- Often others start off confident in their position, but leave the interaction with the passive-aggressive person feeling confused and guilty, but not sure what happened to cause them to feel that way
- A favourite statement is "It's for your own good"
- Has low self-esteem
- "I'm ok, you're not ok"
- The passive-aggressive person's needs get met over the other person's needs

An Assertive person:

- Is direct
- Speaks calmly, clearly and in concrete terms
- Expresses personal opinions, thoughts and feelings

- Non-verbal and verbal messages are congruent
- Considers rights of self and rights of others
- Exhibits honesty, tactfulness, respect
- Is confident
- Makes eye contact
- Uses "I" statements (owns opinions, feelings etc.)
- Takes self-responsibility for their own choices and allows others self-responsibility for theirs
- Has healthy self-esteem
- "I'm ok, you're ok"
- Sometimes the assertive person's needs get met and sometimes the other person's needs get met. A compromise or collaboration may be necessary. Whether their direct needs get met or not, every time assertive individuals express themselves honestly, they validate themselves

Individuals can exhibit all or some of the characteristics listed above. The key difference between assertive communication and the other three styles is that assertive communication is *direct* (clear, concise and to the point), while the others are *indirect* (hinting, mixed messages and avoiding the point). Also, the assertive person tends to have healthy self-esteem while the other three have low self-esteem. Yes, even the aggressive person has low self-esteem although they may appear confident. Think of it this way, why would someone have to control and put down someone else if they felt good about themselves?

Being assertive means being direct, expressing our feelings, thoughts and needs without hinting, playing games, blaming, shaming, or being silent and hoping the other person reads our mind.

We ask for what we want. We state it clearly and concisely. We say it in a respectful way believing that we can deal with the consequences whatever they may be. We don't beat around the bush. We don't numb our feelings by eating or drinking when we are upset instead of expressing our feelings.

An initial step toward becoming assertive is to identify your current styles of communicating.

Where do you see yourself in the above four descriptions? Which of these 4 communication styles do you use most often?

If you use a different style with different people, or in different situations, why do you use that specific communication style at those times?

Our communication styles are learned

We learn our style of communication from the people around us. We learn by observing how others interact with each other. If you had an assertive parent then you are more likely to communicate assertively yourself because you know what it looks like. If a passive parent or an aggressive parent raised you, those are the styles that are most familiar to you and that you are most likely to duplicate. So just as you learned how to be aggressive, passive or passive-aggressive in the past, you can learn to be assertive now.

Think about people in your life both past and present. How would you classify:

- *Your mother's predominant communication style?*

- *Your father's?*

- *Any other adults who raised you?*

- *Your siblings?*

How did these different styles interact within your family? Which ones worked best together? Which ones conflicted?

Who are you most like? Who did you learn your style from?

The four communication styles in relationships

Each of the 4 styles interacts with the other styles in a predictable way. We tend to be attracted to what is familiar and also what allows us to interact in a way that gets our needs met. For example, if people in my family were passive and aggressive, I would tend to be attracted to other people who were passive and aggressive. The relationship dynamics produced by this combination are predictable and familiar to me. Once I recognize this pattern I can start to make changes.

They say opposites attract. In communication styles this can be true. A passive person and an aggressive person in a relationship will compliment each other and the relationship will probably work fine for a while. The aggressive person wants their own way and the passive person will allow them to avoid rocking the boat and causing conflict. These dynamics often work until the passive person hits his or her limit and gets fed up. Then they leave, blow up or perhaps decide to become assertive.

Two passive people in a relationship will never be able to make any decisions. They'll have difficulty even deciding where to go for dinner as each will want to please the other person and let the other one decide. "Where ever you want to go." "No where ever you want to go." "You decide." 'No, you decide. What ever you want." It can feel very frustrating for others to interact with a passive person. The relationship can feel very one-sided.

Alternatively, two aggressive people in a relationship will be knocking heads with both wanting to get their own needs met over the other person. With an aggressive person others can feel left out of the relationship, as though they don't exist and none of their needs matter. Similarly to the passive-passive combination, this relationship can feel very one-sided.

An aggressive or passive-aggressive person will not last long in a relationship with an assertive person. The assertive person will not put up with their manipulating or controlling. In other words the assertive person will not play along with their mind games. The passive-aggressive person tends to seek out relationships with passive people who will be eager players in their games.

However, if one of the other 3 styles wants to change and become more assertive, being in a relationship with an assertive person could facilitate this process. The assertive person would expect direct and honest communication from the other person. They would not be willing to participate in perpetuating the ineffective communication.

Think of your relationships (outside your family) both past and present. This can include spouses, boyfriends, girlfriends, co-workers, and friends. What is your usual communication style in relationships and to whom are you most often attracted?

What is their style? Why do you imagine you are attracted to them?

Think of your relationships that did not work out. What communication style did those people have?

How did their communication style combine effectively or ineffectively with your style?

How do you imagine this might have contributed to the relationship not being successful?

What about the other challenging people in your life – that teacher that you never got along with or that co-worker that challenged everything you did? Where would you place them within the 4 communication styles? What dynamics were created when your communication style interacted with their style?

Testing your communication IQ

Let's see if you can correctly identify the communication styles used in each of the following scenarios. Consider voice tone and how the statement might be said when making your choice.

In the scenarios listed below, choose the communication style that best goes with each response.
A = assertive
AG = aggressive
P = passive
PA = passive-aggressive

1. You have just finished preparing dinner for a friend. He arrives one hour late without letting you know he would be late. You are very upset that he did not call to let you know he would be late.

Your response:

   a. Hi. Come on in. Glad you are here. _____

   b. I am sick and tired of you always being late. You have no consideration for anyone but yourself. _____

   c. I am really angry that you did not call me to tell me that you were going to be late. I would appreciate you calling me to let me know when you expect to get here. _____

2. You are having a disagreement with your partner and she criticizes your appearance and calls you fat.

Your response:

   a. Well you're not any prize yourself. When was the last time you looked in the mirror? _____

   b. I feel hurt when you criticize my appearance and I would appreciate you staying on topic instead of putting me down. _____

   c. I'm sorry. _____

3. You have just received a compliment on your new outfit. You really like it too.

Your response:

   a. Oh, it's nothing. I got it really cheap. _____

   b. Thank you. _____

   c. You like it? I'm surprised you noticed it? But really it's nothing special. _____

4. You are returning a damaged piece of furniture to the department store. You want a replacement item. The clerk has said that the mark is hardly noticeable.

Your response:

   a. Just give me my money. I don't give a damn what you think. _____

   b. Yes. I'd still like to return this one and get another one. _____

   c. Are you sure it is not very noticeable? _____

5. You are going out with a group of friends for dinner and they decide to go to a restaurant that you dislike very much.

Your response:

   a. I don't like the food at that restaurant. How about the Med Grille? _____

   b. Well, if we have to go there fine. I guess I might be able to find something I could eat. _____

   c. Silence. You don't say anything and simply go along with the group. _____

6. Your mother has just called to say that she is coming for a visit this weekend and will be staying with you. You already have plans for the entire weekend that you do not want to break.

Your response:

   a. You're coming here again. Why don't you go visit Anne for a change? _____

   b. I already have plans for this weekend. I'll give you a call next week and we can arrange for another time for you to visit that will work out better for both of us. _____

   c. Oh, okay. Well I'll see you tomorrow. _____

7. You ask a friend to help you move next weekend and they say no that they are not available.

Your response:

   a. Oh sorry. I didn't mean to bug you. Sorry, I shouldn't have asked you. _____

   b. Well great, thanks. What about all those times that I helped you move? _____

   c. Okay. I'll give someone else a call. _____

   d. Oh come on, can't you change your plans? It won't take very long. _____

8. A co-worker keeps asking you to do her work. You are very busy and can hardly get your own work done on time.

Your response:

   a. Forget it. Do your own damn work and stop bugging me. _____

   b. I'm kind of busy. But I guess I can fit it in. __ _____

   c. No Cathy. I don't have time to help you with your work. I have enough of my own work to do. _____

Adapted in part from: Career & College Skills 100, J. Beales.

Answers:

1.   a = passive *(in the scenario description you said you are very upset)*

b = aggressive

c = assertive

2.   a = aggressive

b = assertive

c = passive *(he has insulted you and you are apologizing??)*

3.   a = passive *(you are discounting the compliment and at the same time focusing the attention off of you)*

b = assertive

c = passive-aggressive *("I'm surprised you noticed it." is the portion of the statement that makes the response passive-aggressive.)*

4.   a = aggressive

b = assertive

c = passive

5.   a = assertive

b = passive-aggressive *(you are playing the victim here and pouting)*

c = passive

6.   a = aggressive
        b = assertive
        c = passive

7.   a = passive
        b = passive-aggressive *(you are trying to lay on a guilt trip and you are keeping score)*
        c = assertive
        d = aggressive *(the other person has already said no. You are now trying to control them by not accepting their answer.)*

8.   a = aggressive
        b = passive
        c = assertive

How well did you correctly identify the four communication styles?

What did you notice about the assertive responses? What did they tend to have in common?

The assertive responses tend to be clear, concise and direct. In the next section we will start to focus more closely on what assertive communication sounds like.

Beginning your journey to becoming assertive

You have the right to stand up for yourself and to assert your individuality. You do not have to be assertive all the time, in all circumstances. However, if you are often upset because you are not assertive or always choose to not be assertive, you may be avoiding issues that are important to you. It is often easier to be assertive in certain situations or with certain people than with others. The goal is to be **able** to assert yourself and to be free to decide when to do this.

When you are assertive you remain in control of your actions. You will gradually become more and more assertive without changing your character.

Assertiveness is not winning. You may not get what you want, but you will feel better for stating your point without debating or backing down.

Effective communication and listening skills can help you to be effective in expressing your feelings, thoughts, needs and wants.

Being assertive includes more than words; it also includes voice tone, eye contact, posture and other non-verbal behaviours.

The basic tenets of an assertive philosophy

1.   By standing up for our rights we show we respect ourselves and achieve respect from other people.

2.   By trying to govern our lives so as to never hurt anyone, we end up hurting other people and ourselves.

3.   Sacrificing our rights usually results in destroying relationships or preventing ones from beginning.

4.   Not letting others know how we feel and what we think is a form of selfishness.

5.   Sacrificing our rights usually results in training other people to mistreat us.

6.   If we don't tell other people how their behaviour negatively affects us, we are denying them an opportunity to change their behaviour.

7.   We can decide what's important to us; we do not have to suffer from the "tyranny" of the "should" and "should not".

8.   When we do what we think is right for us, we feel better about ourselves and have more authentic and satisfying relationships with others.

9.   We all have a natural right to courtesy and respect.

10. We all have a right to express ourselves as long as we don't violate the rights of others.

11. There is more to be gained from life by being free and able to stand up for ourselves and from honouring the same rights for other people.

12. When we are assertive everyone involved usually benefits.

Adapted from: Jakubowski-Spector, P. (1977). Self-Assertive Training Procedures For Women

"You create your opportunities by asking for them." Shatki Gawain

2

What Keeps You Non-Assertive?

How did you learn to be non-assertive?

What are some of your life experiences that taught you not to be assertive, which emphasized your passivity or aggression?

We are not born knowing how to communicate in relationships. We learn by observing how those around us communicate with each other. If there was no one who modeled assertiveness for us, then we did not learn how to do it. If we saw other family members responding in a passive or aggressive way, we made the assumptions that this was what was expected of us. Or we decided to behave in the opposite way because of the outcomes we saw from the various interactions.

Some of us were punished when we spoke out so were taught in that way to be passive and be quiet. Others were given messages about expressing themselves, such as "children are to be seen and not heard", "don't cry or I'll give you something to cry about" or "don't be silly, there's nothing to be scared of". You may have been taught that it was conceited or arrogant to put yourself first.

In contrast, other people were taught that the only way to get their needs met or to get attention was to compete and be better than the other person. They learned how to be aggressive and to win.

How did you personally learn to be non-assertive?

How do you keep yourself non-assertive today?

We keep ourselves non-assertive:

- Through our negative self-talk and our belief systems about interacting with others

- By making choices that emphasize others' needs, over our own or our needs exclusively without considering others

- By not taking risks

- By not expressing our true needs, wants, thought and feelings

- By not even knowing what we need, want, think or feel because we are so focused on everyone and everything external to us

- By keeping silent

- By being in relationships with others who encourage us to stay passive or aggressive

- By overly worrying about what others think about us

- By not wanting to disappoint others

- By feeling threatened by others

How do you act non-assertively in your current life?

Do you like assertive people? Do you think people will like you when you are assertive?

People may be surprised and comment on your assertiveness, but that does not mean you acted inappropriately. Sometimes people don't like other people who are assertive. They may think an assertive woman is a bitch or that the person is "full of themselves" and doesn't care about other people. This often is because the recipient of the assertive behaviour is not getting what they want. They can't manipulate the other person. The assertive person is standing up to them and that's not what they want.

This especially occurs when there are dynamics established in the relationship where the now assertive person has been passive in the past. The other non-assertive person resists this newly found assertiveness because it is not what they signed on for when they started the relationship.

When you change how you interact with another person, that person needs to make a decision as to how she will now interact with you. She has the choice to:

- change along with you and embrace the new dynamics
- search out someone new who will interact in the style to which she had grown accustomed
- try to drag you back to how things used to be because your new behaviour is still unfamiliar and your old behaviour is still quite comfortable

How someone responds to your assertiveness is his or her choice. It is up to them to accept it, reject it or be offended by it. We are not responsible for someone else's feelings, actions or decisions. How they respond is completely their choice.

If they do not like your behaviour it is up to them to be assertive with you as well and let you know. Or they need to find some other way to get their needs met. Assertiveness allows flexibility and space for negotiation.

What prevents you from being assertive?

- Fear of other people's responses
- Fear of conflict
- Fear that others will use the information against me
- Don't know how to be assertive
- Don't know what it is
- Don't know that I have the option to be assertive
- It's selfish or uncaring
- My negative self-talk, my belief systems about being assertive
- What I perceive to be the expectations of others

What prevents you personally from being assertive?

Self-esteem and assertiveness

Self-esteem and assertiveness are directly related. If you recall back in the first chapter when we discussed the four styles of communication, the three non-assertive styles of communication (passive, aggressive and passive-aggressive) all had low self-esteem.

If you don't feel good about yourself and believe in yourself, you are more likely to look externally for answers and motivation. If you don't trust yourself, you are less likely to be assertive and express your feelings, needs and wants. You are more likely to try to manipulate and control the situation or others so that the outcome is predictable and something you can cope with. You are less likely to take risks where you don't know the outcome, because you won't trust that you can handle it.

Therefore, improving your self-esteem will help you to be more assertive. Similarly, the positive outcomes from taking the risk to act assertively will help to boost your belief in yourself and boost your self-esteem.

It is important to identify what our blocks are to being assertive, so that in addition to learning the new skills we can also work at clearing away the obstacles to initiating and maintaining these new behaviours.

3

What Do You Believe About Being Assertive?

Our belief systems can get in the way of us behaving assertively. When you develop positive beliefs about being assertive, you are more likely to engage in assertive behaviour and to continue acting assertively in the face of criticism and resistance from others. You are less likely to feel guilty after you have expressed your feelings and opinions or asked for your needs to be met.

What are your beliefs that keep you non-assertive?

- I don't have the right to be assertive
- It's selfish
- It is considered arrogant and conceited
- I will hurt the other person's feelings

- The other person will get angry

- They will take advantage of me

- I need to appear stronger than them

- Others will think I am a bitch

- Others will think I am a wimp

- Others' needs come first

- Children are to be seen and not heard (and this belief is kept in place as an adult)

- It's rude

- I will get in trouble

What are three negative beliefs you personally have about being assertive?

You can increase your ability to be assertive by replacing your non-assertive messages (self-talk) with messages that support assertive behaviour. Such as, "I have the right to be assertive" or "I deserve to make choices that support me".

What are five other positive beliefs that would support you being assertive? Look back at the three negative beliefs you listed above for ideas. Try changing them into positive statements.

Self-talk

Our self-talk influences our feelings and perceptions about what's going on in our lives, and it is these thoughts that ultimately determine how we feel, what we do and how we relate to others. When I refer to self-talk I am referring to the "blah, blah, blah" that goes on in our heads. That which is going on in your head right now as you read this book. Our self-talk can be positive or it can be negative. The positive self-talk we want to reinforce and the negative self-talk we want to reframe into positive statements.

Most of these thoughts are habitual and strengthened by repeated patterns of thinking and past experiences, both positive and negative. We tend to assume they are accurate, seldom stopping to question their validity. Our self-talk develops from our past experiences and what we observe others doing and what we hear them saying.

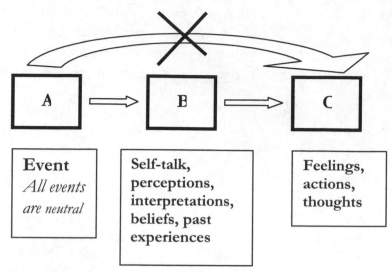

Figure 2

As shown in Figure 2 above, events (A) do not determine our feelings, actions or thoughts (C). All events are neutral until we place a meaning on them or interpret them based on our past experiences and our perception of the world around us. These perceptions are then perpetuated by our self-talk (the blah, blah, blah that goes on in our heads).

Our self-talk (B) determines our feelings, actions and thoughts. We do not have control over the events around us, but we do have control over our thoughts and our perceptions of these events. In Figure 2, A does not cause C; A is followed immediately by B which then determines C.

For example, one woman's husband tells her that he wants a divorce. She responds by feeling sad, hurt and disappointed. She may have said to herself that it was all her fault that she should have tried harder and that she will probably be alone now for the rest of her life ("blah, blah, blah"). A second woman's husband also tells her that he wants a divorce. She is relieved and thankful that it is over. She may have said to herself that she is glad that one of them finally took the step. Now they can get on with their lives.

The initial event is the same in each situation, but each woman's response is unique based on what she says to herself. She cannot change what her husband decided to do, but she can change how she reacts to it.

Whether you are assertive or not is dependent on what you say to yourself at that time. Your self-talk can be supportive and encouraging or it can be negative and self-defeating. We want to maximize the positive self-talk and minimize the negative. Below are the steps to start changing your negative self-talk to positive self-affirming talk.

Steps to improving your self-talk

1. Notice the negative things you say to yourself, either out loud or in your head. Have friends let you know when you are being critical or negative of yourself or a situation. Become aware of what you say to

yourself during stressful situations.

You cannot change something you are not aware you are doing. Becoming aware of your negative self-talk is one of the most difficult aspects of replacing it.

2. Identify where this thought came from. Often they are things that someone said to us in the past. Whose voice have you heard say this before? Are they accurate?

    Even though you think it is your own voice you hear, remind yourself that no baby is born thinking this way. You learned it from someone. Once you identify whose voice it is, it often becomes apparent why that other person might think that way. But do you actually believe this thought or do you just think you should.

3. Challenge these beliefs. Dispute the reality of them. Find one example of an event, person or characteristic that does not fit this belief. Ask yourself or an impartial friend: "Is this thought accurate?", "Is it true?"

    Decide which of these beliefs still fit your life as it is today. Keep the ones that do, eliminate the ones that do not.

4. Replace these negative statements with positive statements or reframe your self-talk with a statement, which more accurately reflects the truth. (i.e. "I have the right to express my feelings".)

5. As you start to do this you may hear other negative self-talk disputing these positive statements. Listen to these voices and use the above steps to dispute these as well. Your self-talk gives you information on your beliefs about your Self. These will be uncovered layer by layer.

6. Continue the above steps over and over as needed. It will take time to replace your negative self-talk and change your beliefs. Be patient and persistent. These negative beliefs were learned and new beliefs can also be learned. Make a point of also changing behaviours or choices that perpetuate the beliefs that you want to eliminate.

Make a list of the negative beliefs that you have about being assertive. Work through the 6 steps above and replace your negative self-talk with positive self-talk, such as "It is okay for me to say no", "I have the right to express my opinion".

Create your own positive reality by using
positive self-talk regularly and frequently to
encourage you to be assertive and stand up for
yourself.

The world does not revolve around you

It is our belief systems that often get in our way of
being assertive. One belief that often prevents us from
being assertive is that we are responsible for other
people's feelings and for what happens in their lives.
Other people are responsible for their own feelings and
choices; we are not. I will discuss this further
throughout this book.

I thank my friend G. for a comment that became a
catalyst for changing how I perceived the world. I was
talking to him on the phone one day and he sounded
irritated and angry. We talked for quite awhile and after
I hung up, as I tended to do at that time, I obsessed
about what I had said to make him angry. Then I
worried that he didn't like me any more, that I had
screwed up ("blah, blah, blah"). I was very good at
continuing my conversations for hours afterward
without ever involving the other person and obsessing
and analyzing and, and, and…

But on this rare occasion I had the nerve to call him back. How I got the nerve I don't know. And I said to him, "You were so angry on the phone. I'm sorry. What did I say wrong?" His response was, **"The world does not revolve around you, Barb. I had a bad day at work!"**

On the outside I simply said, "Oh". On the inside, I was shocked. I thought I don't think that way. I don't think the world revolves around me. I'm always worrying about what everyone else is thinking and feeling. Worrying about whether they are all right. Worrying about whether I had offended them. But the question is, "Why do I worry about that?" So that I don't do anything to offend them. To make sure they are happy. To make sure they will still like me. So it was all about me.

I was shocked by this realization. I felt selfish. I thought I was supposed to be worried about everyone else. That if I didn't ensure they were happy, they wouldn't like me. I struggled with this insight, but it really was a catalyst for me to start taking a look at my own behaviours and choices from a different perspective.

The bottom line is that the whole world does not revolve around you, but your world does. Most people could care less about what you are doing with your life. They are more concerned about what they are doing with their own life and whether you are looking at them or judging them.

It took me a while to figure out why this realization bothered me so much. I came to the awareness that I needed to think that others cared about what I did with my life and about me because if they didn't who would? I sure didn't at the time. I was so busy worrying about everyone else.

"The world does not revolve around you." I still remind myself of this and I share this insight with most of my clients and in almost all of my workshops. We are not as all powerful as we may think we are. Our choices and actions do not impact the <u>whole</u> world. They do impact <u>our</u> world. So when I am worried about what to say to someone. When I am over-analyzing a past conversation. When I am making assumptions about someone else's actions or feelings and making it all about me, I remind myself, **"The world does not revolve around me."**

Are you afraid of appearing selfish?

Taking care of our own needs and expressing ourselves does not mean that we are being selfish. For many people the word "selfish" has a very negative connotation.

I like to say we are being "self-full". Our needs and other people's needs are not always mutually exclusive. Just because we make choices for ourselves does not mean that we will always choose to ignore others and not do anything for them. But we will do it from a place of choice rather than a place of "have to" or fear.

Sometimes when we always step up and do something for someone else, when perhaps we don't want to, we may be preventing them from seeking out the help they need from someone else who might be more qualified or more able to meet their needs. It can also be detrimental to that other person because when we always do it for them; we are preventing them from learning to do it for themselves. So instead of thinking of being assertive as being selfish, think of it as respecting our rights and the rights of others to make personal choices for ourselves.

Below is a *Bill of Assertive Rights* created by Manuel Smith in his book "When I Say No I Feel Guilty". This is a list of rights that all of us have. If we acknowledge them, they will help us be more assertive and stand up for ourselves when others are not supporting our assertiveness.

A bill of assertive rights

1. You have the right to judge your own behaviour, thoughts, and emotions.

2. You have the right to offer no reasons or excuses for justifying your behaviour.

3. You have the right to decide if you are responsible for finding solutions to other people's problems.

4. You have the right to change your mind.

5. You have the right to make mistakes – and be responsible for them.

6. You have the right to say, "I don't know."

7. You have the right to be independent of the goodwill of others.

8. You have the right to be illogical in making decisions.

9. You have the right to say, "I don't understand."

10. You have the right to say, "I don't care."

11. You have the right to have needs and to have those needs be as important as others' needs.

12. You have the right to ask other people to respond to your needs.

13. You have the right to have feelings and to express these feelings in ways, which do not violate the dignity of other people.

14. You have the right to decide whether you'll meet other people's expectations or whether you'll act in ways which fit you, as long as you act in ways which don't violate other people's rights.

15. You have the right to say no without feeling guilty.

Which of these rights do you currently recognize in your life?

Which ones are totally absent from your life?

Which ones do you recognize in others but not yourself?

> *"Assertiveness is not what you do, it's who you are."* Cal Le Mon

4

What are Your Obstacles to Becoming Assertive?

Feelings, they're nothing more than feelings.

One of the number one reasons people give for not being assertive is that they don't want to upset the other person. They are focused on taking care of the other person's feelings, but willing to neglect their own.

I find that in our society we are so afraid of what we deem as "negative emotions" such as anger, sadness, disappointment or fear to name a few, that we do everything possible to avoid feeling them or to avoid provoking them in someone else. I hear from clients, "I can't tell him that, he'll be disappointed" or "she'll be mad because she doesn't approve of my choice". These statements are made with the unspoken thought that "obviously, I can't do what I planned to do because I have to ensure the other person is not upset."

Feelings are natural. They are simply energy that needs to be expressed in some way. They are also transient and change throughout the day several times. We wake up and feel happy, then we stub our toe and feel grumpy, then our cat wants a cuddle and we cheer up, then we find out we didn't win the lottery again and we feel disappointed, and then realize it's Friday and we feel good again etc. We experience a multitude of feelings over one day.

One friend told me a story about how upset her grandfather was that she were marrying someone of another religion and that her mother was so completely focused on the fact that her father was upset, that she almost had her daughter cancel her wedding. Her mother kept saying, "But my father's upset. It's so terrible. We can't have this continue." There was such fear of the negative feeling that the grandfather was experiencing that all the energy got redirected on to how to make him happy.

I said, "Yes, he's upset. Okay. It doesn't automatically mean something has to be done to change that." He has the right to be upset and he has the right to not want her to marry the man. And the granddaughter has the right to want to marry him. Both views can exist at the same time and the grandfather will choose to move through his feelings or not.

You can't make someone feel a certain way.

You are not responsible for how someone else feels. You behave in a certain way and the other person chooses how they respond – even if it is an unconscious choice. For example, if two of you were to ask me to go out to a movie on Friday and I said "no" to both of you, one person may respond by feeling embarrassed for asking me, blaming herself, feeling like it was a dumb thing to do. While the other person may simply say, "Fine, that's too bad you're not available. I'll call you next week."

I responded the same way to both people. Their individual responses are based on their own individual beliefs and their self-talk in response to my refusal. When we try to predict how someone will respond it is often a projection of how we would respond in the same situation. So if you are afraid to speak to someone because you feel responsible for their response, you are not allowing them the self-responsibility for their own response and are in a sense trying to control them.

At the same time this also means that we have to take responsibility for our own feelings and not blame other people for our responses. For example, "He _made_ me angry" is not accurate. He responded in a certain way and your response was anger. Someone else may have responded differently. You are responsible for your response of anger. He did not cause it. Blaming others for our feelings can cause us to feel powerless.

You are discounting yourself when you try to protect the other person's feelings by not expressing your own.

Being assertive does not necessarily mean that we always get what we want. Just as we have the right to ask for what we want, the other person has the right to say no or to negotiate. Assertiveness is not about power over others. It is about acknowledging and validating ourselves. By simply taking the risk to express our thoughts and feelings, we are validating ourselves. We are saying that we have the right to think or feel this way even if no one else agrees.

When we hide our thoughts and feelings and instead always put others first we are discounting ourselves. What we are implying is that we don't want the other person to be upset, but that it is okay for us to feel hurt and ignored. Why might that be? Hmmm…

The intention of being assertive is not to always get your needs met. It is to validate and acknowledge *yourself* by expressing them.

Making someone else happy

You are not responsible for ensuring that someone else is happy. If they have made a choice and find themselves in a situation in which they are unhappy, it is up to them to choose to change it.

I often hear from people how they are feeling so sad and guilty when they are unable to cheer up their friend who is unhappy about his new job or his relationship or his home or... They are stressing themselves out and are unhappy themselves because they have taken on the responsibility to make the other person's life better. Instead of asking "what can I do to make him feel better?" instead ask "what does my response to his feelings tell me about myself?"

The other person may choose to do nothing about his situation and that is his choice. If you are always in his life trying to fix it, he may never make the effort to do it himself. And what will he do when you are not there?

What's the worse thing that could happen?

When a client is hesitant to be assertive because of the fear of how another person will respond, I will often ask them, "What is the worse thing that could happen?" Once they identify that, I ask them if they think that they can cope with that outcome. I ask them what they think is the likelihood of that outcome happening.

Usually what we imagine in our heads is always worse than what actually could happen.

For example, you tell me you fear that your mother will never talk to you again when you tell her that you won't come to her place for Christmas. I would ask you, *"What's the worse thing that you think could happen if you told her?"*

Your answer may be that she won't talk to you again. I would then ask, *"What is the likelihood that she will never talk to you again"*.

You may reply with, "Well, she probably will give me the silent treatment". Next I would ask, *"How long do you think that would last?"*

"Oh, probably not long". So in other words she'll likely get over it.

Yes, and then what?

When I teach assertiveness skills or when I am with a client who is interested in becoming assertive I also use the statement "yes and then what" when they are resistant to being assertive with someone because they are afraid of the outcome.

"Yes and then what" helps them to see past what they imagine the initial outcome to be which prevents them from speaking up for themselves. This question helps them to follow through and see that the potential negative reaction will not last forever.

For example, "I can't tell my sister that I don't want to hear her negative comments about how I take care of my child because my sister will be angry". *Yes, and then what?*

"She will be upset and not talk to me". *Yes, and then what?*

"She won't call me and will tell my mom how horrible I was". *Yes, and then what?*

"I probably won't hear from her for weeks". *Yes, and how long do you think she will not talk to you?*

"Oh, probably until she needs something from me or is upset at my other sister about something."

The "yes, and then what" question helps us to recognize that behaviour changes over time and that the initial reaction we anticipate is just one rest stop along the way, but not the end. Yes, her sister may be angry and that is a normal response. It will pass. She doesn't have to panic and forsake her needs and her feelings.

Whose problem is it anyway?

Often we resist being assertive and complain that the other person should be making the changes instead. "Why does it always have to be me? Shouldn't they stop doing that? Shouldn't they know better? Shouldn't THEY...?"

What we are really saying is that it would be a whole lot easier if the other person made the changes. Then we wouldn't have to make the effort or take the risk to do it ourselves.

Obviously it isn't their issue or they would be the one complaining about it and wanting it to change. But they aren't, you are. And if it is your issue, then you need to speak up and make the change yourself. Maybe the other person is not worried about the situation or isn't even aware it is a problem.

If you want something in your life to change it is up to you to take the steps necessary to make it happen. I invite you to ask yourself, *"What is the actual issue here?"* *"Whose issue is this?"* *"Whose problem is this?"*. Is it the other person who has a problem or is it you who would like to see the situation change?

If you don't tell them, they may not know that what they are doing is bothering you.

If we don't speak up to others and let them know that we are unhappy or hurt by something they have said or done, we don't offer them the opportunity to change. This comes from the assumption that they would not choose to make those changes. Actually they might truly want to and may be sad that they have been unknowingly behaving in a way that was distressing to us.

When we postpone telling them how we are feeling we can begin to hold a grudge that will most likely come out in our behaviour toward them and become a stressor in our relationship. By telling them how we feel, we could resolve it before this happens.

What you are trying to prevent from happening by controlling a situation usually ends up happening anyway.

For example, I may not tell my friend how I feel about a situation or express my opinion because I don't want to upset her or cause hurt feelings. But if I was to take a good look at the friendship, what I'm trying to avoid is probably already happening.

I may be hurt and upset because my friend doesn't seem to understand me, yet I haven't ever told her the details necessary to understand me. She doesn't know that I am feeling hurt and upset, but is likely picking up unconsciously (non-verbally) that something is not right. As a result, she is worrying about me and worried about our friendship. What I was trying to avoid happening is happening already.

Or I don't tell my partner that I am worried that we are growing apart because I don't want to rock the boat or take the chance of making him angry. Instead I hold back my feelings and withdraw. This behaviour likely causes more conflict and more distance in my relationship. So my partner gets upset and what I have been trying to avoid happens anyway.

Others read our behaviour, even if we don't speak up.

Our friends often already know what is happening for us even when we haven't verbally told them. So when we do speak up, it is usually not a surprise.

My friends knew I was pouting in the other room even though I would keep saying I was all right. And when I finally had the awareness and courage to tell my friends in Toronto that I realized I had always been so angry about my life and my relationships, they said they knew that all along and were simply waiting for me to take the risk to tell them. At first I was pissed off that they didn't approach me and ask me how I was feeling, to help me deal with my anger. But looking back I probably would have denied it and said I was doing just fine. There was no way I was going to *directly* express my anger at that point in my life. Instead I pouted, was controlling, sarcastic, or over ate to *indirectly* deal with my anger.

Being assertive is a choice.

You can choose to be assertive in a situation or you can choose not to be. But if you choose never to be assertive then I would question whether you could be assertive if you wanted to.

In some situations you may choose not to be assertive because it is not in your best interest. For example, you may choose not to be assertive with a boss who in the past has fired someone who stood up to her and right now possibly losing your job is not a risk that you are willing to take. It is important that you recognize that you are making a choice to do this and that you are not trapped in the situation.

When we make a choice to do, or to not do, something it is because we have decided that we are willing to deal with the consequences or outcome. We believe that we are able to do so.

When you finally do make the choice to be assertive remember how good it feels. You can use that positive feeling as motivation in the future when you are faced again with the decision of whether to be assertive or not.

If not now, when?

When I was resistant to taking the risk to be assertive, I often reminded myself of the quotes "if you always do what you've always done, you'll always get what you always got" and "if not now, when?" When will it ever be a better time to take the risk?

It can be a relief to get it over with by finally being assertive. You can experience the short-term pain of plunging in and taking the risk to be assertive versus experiencing the long-term pain of being miserable and frustrated with staying passive. If I don't deal with a specific situation now, the situation usually escalates and is harder to deal with later. The more we believe that we can deal with the consequences or outcomes of our actions the more likely we are to take risks and step out of our comfort zone. When we believe in ourselves and our ability to adapt and respond to the unknown, the easier it is to validate ourselves and express our thoughts and feelings.

That's their choice.

Being assertive also involves allowing the other person the freedom and responsibility to make their own choices, whether we agree with them or not. The choices they make in their lives are their choices to make, not ours.

We usually don't want them telling us how to feel or

how to live our life so we need to give them the same respect and trust that they will make the choices they need to make. We need to trust that they will deal with the outcomes whether positive or negative. Even though we may think differently, they are the best judges about their own lives.

Instead of focusing on them, focus your attention back on yourself and ask yourself, *"What motivates me to try to tell other people how to live their lives?"* Spending our energy trying to control other people's lives allows us to avoid looking at our own lives. It is a whole lot less painful for me to focus on how someone else should change then to do it myself. They are the ones who will be making the effort and who will be dealing with the consequences of that change.

I think also that sometimes we work on getting others to change to see if it can be done and how it can be done before we take the risk to make a similar change ourselves. Let them stumble and fall so that I can avoid tripping.

Making excuses

When we think we must justify saying "no" to or make excuses for why we are late etc, our excuses are usually more for us than for anyone else. Giving excuses for our choices is usually a way of giving ourselves permission for what we are doing. We are often trying to reduce our guilt or make ourselves feel better. Most of the time the other person doesn't care why. They simply want to move on and call someone else or look elsewhere to get their needs met. Also the more elaborate your excuse is the more ammunition the other person has to manipulate and use against you if they are so inclined!

Is there room for you in your life?

If you are always taking care of everyone else and always worried about what everyone else is thinking, then you will likely not have much time to take care of yourself. When all your energy is focused externally, you will have little time to figure out what you want, need or think. Remember my mantra I mentioned in the introduction, *"What about me, what do I want?"* Turn your attention back on yourself so you can make the best choices for you.

It's not good, bad, right or wrong.
It just is.

Remind yourself that your feelings and needs are not good, bad, right or wrong. They just are. We will often hold back if we are judging ourselves negatively. Stay in the present and accept your feelings for what they are: simply energy that needs to be released in some way.

Which of these obstacles seem most familiar to you? Which ones are blocking you from becoming assertive?

What can you say to yourself when you find yourself blocked by one of these obstacles?

What else stood out for you from this chapter?

What about me, what do I want?

5

What Else Do I Need to Know About Becoming Assertive?

Assertiveness can be people-specific and/or situation-specific.

If you are assertive in one area of your life it means that you <u>know how</u> to be assertive. If at the same time you are not assertive in another area, the question to ask yourself is:

What is stopping me from being assertive in these other areas of my life?

Often it is our beliefs that determine whether or not we are assertive in a particular situation or with a particular group of people. Some people find it easier to be assertive with strangers while others find it easier to be assertive with family members or friends. In each situation it is because of that particular person's past experiences and resulting beliefs.

Take a look at the people or situations in which you are least likely to be assertive and ask yourself:

"Why am I unable to be assertive in this situation but can when I…?"

"What am I afraid of?"

I suggest that when you practice your new assertiveness skills that you do so with someone or in a situation, where you feel safest and less threatened. Don't start with the scariest situation. Practice, practice, practice first. When you take the risk to be assertive and it works, remember what that feels like and use this as motivation for next time when you are timid or resistant to taking the risk.

Assertion self-assessment table

To help identify the specific people or specific situations where you find it most difficult to be assertive, complete the *Assertion Self-Assessment Table* on the following page

Each column represents a different group of people and the rows represent different situations. The purpose of the chart is for you to determine how often you are able to respond assertively in each of the situations (rows) and with each group of people (columns).

Using the scale: *1 = usually, 2 = sometimes, 3 = seldom or never,* place a number in each of the squares in the table. The squares that are shaded do not need to be completed. If struggling with a response, think of how you would most likely respond with that group of people in that situation.

While you are completing the chart, pay attention to your self-talk.

What are you __thinking__ when you consider behaving that way with that particular group of people?

What are you __feeling__ when you consider behaving that way with that particular group of people?

Once you have completed the chart. Notice the columns and rows where you have mainly 3's. If you do not have many 3's, notice the columns or rows where you have mainly 2's. Consider the following questions:

What patterns do you notice?

What behaviours are hardest for you to do assertively? Why? What is it about each of those behaviours?

What groups are hardest for you to be assertive with? Why? What is it about each of those groups of people?

What is your negative self-talk when answering these questions? What you say to yourself is a valuable source of information.

Do you have any 1's on your chart or, if not, do you have any 2's? Most people have 1's or 2's in at least a few boxes. Congratulations, this indicates that you <u>know</u>

how to be assertive because you are doing so during these times.

Why are you able to be assertive in these situations or with these people, but not at the other times?

Try not to discount the times when you <u>are</u> able to be assertive by minimizing them or assuming that anyone could be assertive then. The bottom line is regardless of the reason it shows you that <u>you can be assertive under the right conditions</u>. You can learn from this information and use it to help change your negative self-talk that is preventing you from being assertive the rest of the time. You can also use this information as reinforcement that you are <u>able</u> to be assertive. Remember how you respond (what you say, how you act) in those situations. This is what being assertiveness looks and sounds like.

Assertion Self-Assessment Table

Persons

Assertive behaviours	Same sex friends	Opposite sex friends	Spouse, boyfriend, girlfriend, partner	Parents, family members, siblings	Children	Bosses, teachers, authority figures	Waiters, salespersons, bus drivers	Coworkers, colleagues, staff
Give compliments								
Receive compliments								
Ask for help								
Express liking, love								
Initiate and maintain conversations								
Stand up for my rights								
Refuse requests from others, say no								
Express opinions								
Express anger								

Adapted from: Galassi & Galassi. (1977). Assert Yourself!

What about me, what do I want?

This is the mantra that I said in my head when I was trying to learn to focus on myself and not spend so much time focusing on what everyone else was thinking or feeling. At that time, I could have told you what I thought I <u>should</u> want, or what I thought <u>you wanted</u> to hear, but I was unable to tell you what I genuinely wanted, thought or felt. Either I didn't know or I was too afraid to know in case it caused conflict in some way.

The messages I received growing up were to put other people first. I learned about how I needed to be in order to be liked, to be loved, and to get my needs met. One major example of these messages developed from my family's reaction to me being teased at school about being overweight. They suggested that if I lost weight I wouldn't be teased. Although I recognize now that my parents' intentions were for me to fit in and be accepted, I interpreted the message to be that there was something wrong with me and that it was okay for those other kids and adults to judge and tease me. As a result, I became very focused on trying to please others and make them like me even if it required changing or denying who I was.

As children we are dependent on the adults around us for survival. So we put up our little antennas and we figure out how we need to be in order for the adults around us to love us and take care of us. This may not be how we actually feel or think. If we are brought up in a house where we were abused, neglected, or simply had our feelings discounted and were told how to feel or think, then for survival we learned quickly how to behave in order to be taken care of.

For example, if I felt angry, and I have been told, "that good girls don't get angry." I can't assume that my parents are wrong, because for my sense of security I need to believe that they know what they are doing. Instead, I assume that there must be something wrong with me and I stuff my anger (even though anger is simply a natural response to feeling threatened or my needs not getting met) and I figure out how I need to be in order for my parents to continue to love me.

As a result of this we can end up developing several aspects of our Self - *an inner self, a private self* and *a public self*. My *inner self* is the part of me that is authentic – how I truly feel or think. But if I am brought up in an environment where I am told that what I feel doesn't matter, my feelings are ignored or discounted with comments, such as "don't cry or I'll give you something to cry about", "don't be silly there's nothing to be scared about", or "good girls don't get angry", I learn to stuff these feelings. I figure out how I need to be in order to be loved and accepted. I create a *public self* that is all the characteristics that I have learned are acceptable to others. I numb my *inner self* and I show my *public self* to those I am in relationship with.

In addition, my *private self* is the part of me that I acknowledge but don't show to others. For example, I used to hear from people all the time that I was always so happy and together. When I heard that I thought, "You don't know what I do when I go home at night. This was during the 20 years when I was an active compulsive overeater.

> **"It is better to be hated for what you are, then to be loved for what you are not."**
> **Author unknown**

My compulsive overeating helped me keep my *private self* hidden from others and my *inner self* hidden from me because I was taught that part of me was not ok. Healing came when I integrated my three selves. I acknowledged my *inner self* and let others see all aspects of me including my *private self*. I became one whole self. This did not mean that I showed everybody everything all the time, but I decided what I shared from a place of choice rather than from a place of fear or having to.

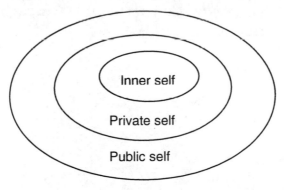

Therefore, one of the first steps toward becoming assertive is to start to identify what you are feeling, thinking and wanting and then to be able to communicate these to the other people in your life.

I started this process by asking myself in each situation, *"what about me, what do I want?"* This encouraged me to take the time to focus inward. In the beginning it wasn't easy for me to even answer this question. Then when my awareness increased I was able to identify some of my needs and wants. Of course, this didn't mean that I did anything about the information and I sure didn't express it to anyone else. But at least I was starting to give a voice to my needs, even if I was the only one to hear it.

Over time as I continued to ask myself, *"what about me, what do I want"* and as my awareness came more easily, I began to take the risk to be assertive and communicate my needs and wants to other people. Eventually I no longer needed to ask myself this question, it became automatic.

What about you, what do you want? How would you like your life to be different?

One of the first steps toward becoming assertive is to figure out what your needs, wants, opinions, thoughts and feelings are. You can't communicate to others what you can't communicate to yourself first.

Ideas to keep in mind

1. Assertive behaviour is often confused with aggressive behaviour. Assertiveness does not involve hurting the other person, physically or emotionally.

2. Assertive behaviour is not about winning it is about respect.

3. Remember: other individuals have a right to respond to your assertiveness with their own wants, needs, feelings, and ideas.

4. By behaving assertively, you open the way for honest and open relationships with others.

6

How Do I Become Assertive?

How assertive are you already?

The following list identifies situations you will likely be faced with at various times in your life. Indicate with a check mark in which of these situations you generally respond assertively. The list can also act as examples of what assertive behaviour looks like.

Situations	Respond Assertively
1. Asking for help	
2. Stating a difference of opinion	
3. Receiving and expressing "negative" feelings	
4. Receiving and expressing "positive" feelings	

5.	Dealing with someone who refuses to cooperate	
6.	Speaking up about something that annoys you	
7.	Saying "no"	
8.	Responding to undeserved criticism	
9.	Making requests of an authority figure	
10.	Asking for something you want	
11.	Proposing a new idea	
12.	Asking questions	
13.	Responding to attempts to make you feel guilty	
14.	Asking for service	
15.	Asking for favours	
16.	Initiating conversations	
17.	Ending a conversation	
18.	Talking about yourself and what you are doing	
19.	Accepting compliments	
20.	Reminding someone of their agreement to do something	

In those above situations where you did not act assertively, how did you respond?

What is it about each of these situations that prevented you from responding assertively?

Which of your beliefs stops you from being assertive in these situations?

Tips to expressing yourself assertively

1. Be clear within yourself as to what you want and what you want to say.

2. Communicate your needs without excuses or disclaimers at the beginning, such as "well, this may not really be important" or "I may be making a big deal out of nothing".

3. Speak clearly and concisely. Speak in a firm and calm voice.

4. Be direct and avoid hinting. If you have a sore back and want a back rub, ask for it. Simply complaining about having a sore back may not achieve your goal of getting a back rub.

5. Describe the particular behaviour or situation as it has occurred and how you would like it to be different.

6. Express your feelings without judgment or justification.

7. Use "I" statements.

8. Maintain eye contact.

Remember it's not just WHAT you say, but also HOW you say it.

The beginnings of assertive communication

When you first are assertive it can be challenging to come up with how to say what you want to say using words that are assertive. The wording is unfamiliar. I have listed below some suggestions that you might use. This is certainly not an exhaustive list, but simply some options to help start you off.

- I don't want to…
- I feel uncomfortable about…

- I'd like to think about it.
- I have an issue I want to talk to you about.
- I don't appreciate that…
- I see it differently.
- I have a problem with that.
- I need help with….
- I feel…
- I think…
- That's not acceptable.
- It is important to me.
- I'm not interested.
- In my opinion…
- I'd like to make a suggestion.
- Perhaps…
- No, thank you.
- Yes, I do mind.
- I don't like that…
- This is what I need.
- Not right now, thank you.
- I'd rather not.
- I think we should discuss this.
- I understand your point of view and…
- I don't have time.
- I don't know.

- No.
- I misunderstood you.
- When are you available to talk about this?
- This is difficult for me to say.
- I would like to…
- I disagree.
- I would rather talk about this later.
- I need some help with…
- I don't understand.

Sample assertive responses

Below are some sample scenarios and corresponding assertive responses to help reinforce further what assertive communication sounds like.

Scenario 1:

One of your parents keeps phoning to complain about your sister's behaviour. You are tired of hearing about the mistakes your sister has made. This happens on a regular basis.

Assertive response:

"Dad, please talk to Carol directly about your concerns. I can't do anything to change her behaviour."

Scenario 2:

Your partner hates the job she is working at and complains continually about how unhappy she is, but never does anything about it. You do not want to hear about it anymore.

Assertive response:

"Mary, I understand that you are very unhappy at your job and we have been talking about it for months. I just don't want to hear about it anymore."

Scenario 3:

You are in a hurry to get to an appointment and someone with a full basket of groceries butts into the line in front of you at the checkout counter.

Assertive response:

"Excuse me, I was standing in line and you butted in front of me. Please move to the end of the line."

Scenario 4:

Some good friends have just phoned to say they are coming to visit for a week and want to stay with you. You don't want to have company that week.

Assertive response:

"Bill, it will be great to see you and Lynne again. It won't work for us to have you stay at our house while you are in town. I would be glad to give you the name of some nearby hotels to phone."

<u>Scenario 5:</u>

You are self-employed and a potential new client is complaining about your professional fees being too high. You are not willing to reduce your fees.

Assertive response:

"I hear from you that my fees are higher than what you hoped to pay. Those fees are what I regularly charge. If you change your mind or would like further information about my services, please feel free to call me again.

Tips for dealing with challenging situations

Saying "no"

One of the words that participants in my assertiveness workshops tell me is the biggest challenge for them is the word "no". For many saying "no" without feeling guilty is impossible. For others, simply saying the word seems impossible. They don't want to hurt the other person's feelings. They don't want them to be angry or disappointed.

On some level I think we believe that if we say "no" we will end up being alone. And at the same time we act as though we believe we are the only person available to say "yes".

When we say "yes" but really want to say "no", the other person can tell. Our body language lets them know. For example, we say "yes" to helping them move when we would rather be going to the art show and our silence, frustration, irritability, sighing, being late, whining etc tells the person that we really don't want to be there. We punish them when it is not their fault that we are doing something we don't want to do.

When we say "yes" to something when we really want to say "no", we prevent the other person from finding someone else to help him or her who might be a better person for the job.

At age two most toddlers have no problem saying "no, no, no, no" to everything. Somewhere along the way we develop beliefs about the negative consequences of saying this simple word. Many of us learned from childhood that saying "no" to certain people was wrong.

Below are some statements about the word no for you to consider:

1. If you don't feel you can also say "no" in a situation, then your "yes" is a lie. You don't feel you have any other options to choose from.

2. "No" is a complete sentence.

3. If you say "no" and someone keeps trying to convince you to change your mind, then they are now trying to control you. The same applies when you do this.

4. You can say "no" without giving excuses. Excuses are so we feel better. If someone invites us to their party and we say no we can't come, they probably don't really care why. They just want to continue on with phoning the other people on their list. Also, the more excuses and justifications that we give them the more ammunition the other person now has to try to control us and talk us into changing our mind.

5. When you say, "yes" to something, you are saying "no" to something else. For example, when I say "yes" to working late or "yes" to being on another committee, I may be saying "no" to spending time with my children or "no" to time for me to relax and practice some self-care. Next time you say "yes" to something or someone, especially when you are feeling pressured to say "yes", ask yourself *"by saying 'yes' to this, what am I saying 'no' to?"*

Many people feel guilty when they say "no". In fact one of the main books in this field from the 1970's is called "When I say no I feel guilty" by Manuel Smith. Others can only make us feel guilty if there is a part of us that feels guilty already.

Imagine a time when you felt really confident about a decision or a choice. Another person probably couldn't make you feel guilty at that point no matter what they did. But if there were a small part inside you that was already feeling guilty then the other person's comments would latch onto that and emphasize that guilt.

I think guilt is our way of feeling like we are doing something without really doing anything. It allows us to feel like we are being good while doing something that we judge as wrong or not appropriate.

Others have the right to say "no" and then it is up to us to get our needs met elsewhere.

Just because you are assertive and ask for your needs to get met does not mean that the other person has to say "yes". Just as you have the right to be assertive the other person also have the right to be assertive and say "no". It does not mean that you were wrong in asking. It simply means that you will need to find another way to get your needs met.

Take the risk to say no to someone today. Start with someone that you feel safe doing so with.

Practice saying no out loud. Be aware of your self-talk when you say it. What negative thoughts go through your head in response to saying no?

"Learn to say 'no' to the good, so you can say, 'yes' to the best."   John C. Maxwell

Setting boundaries

Being assertive includes setting personal boundaries with other people. A boundary is a limit that defines you as separate from others, defines your individuality. Boundaries occur on a continuum from diffuse to flexible (healthy) to rigid. Boundaries separate us from others physically and emotionally and are essential for developing healthy relationships. As we learn to strengthen our boundaries, we gain a clearer sense of our relationships and ourselves. Boundaries allow us to determine how we will allow others to treat us.

Being assertive includes setting personal boundaries with other people. No one can cross your boundaries unless you let them. When we set our boundaries with another person it is up to us to enforce them when the other person attempts to cross them or ignore them. We cannot blame the other person as it is up to us to take personal responsibility to reestablish our boundaries as often as we need to. Others are not always going to be happy when we set our boundaries, but that does not mean that we do not have the right to set them.

We teach others how to treat us. When others treat us badly it is often because we are allowing them to do so by not setting our boundaries, reinforcing them and being assertive. If we treat ourselves badly by not respecting our own needs, then others may see this as an invitation to do so as well. Others cannot control us if we don't allow ourselves to be controlled. Others cannot take away our personal power unless we permit them to do so by the choices that we make.

Below are some tips for setting boundaries:

1. When you need to set a boundary do it clearly, preferably without anger, and in as few words as possible.

2. Avoid justifying, rationalizing or apologizing.

3. Anger, complaining, fear and whining are all clues that you may need to set a boundary.

4. We cannot set a boundary and take care of another person's feelings at the same time.

5. Examine your own beliefs about setting boundaries. It will be difficult to set one if you don't feel that it is okay to do so.

6. Aim for firm, yet flexible, boundaries.

What is a boundary that you have either recently set or would like to set?

What happened, or do you think would happen, if you didn't set this boundary?

What happened, or do you think would happen, if you did set this boundary?

What feelings did/would you have when setting this boundary?

What beliefs do you have about setting boundaries? For example, "if I say no, people won't like me".

Accepting compliments

Many people feel quite uncomfortable when they receive a compliment. It can feel uncomfortable especially if you don't feel good about yourself or if you have been taught that it is conceited or arrogant to speak well of yourself. It can be easier to discount the compliment than to change your negative self-image. Some people may not trust the compliment, thinking the other person wants something from them.

Our response to a compliment can often be an attempt to get the attention off us and reflect it back on to the other person. When someone gives you a compliment you just need to say, "thank you". You don't need to discount it or invalidate what they have said. Expect there to be silence, because in our society we are taught to return a compliment with minimizing ("this old thing") or redirecting it ("oh, you look great too") or discounting and focusing on the negative ("oh, but I could have done better"). When you respond this way you are negating the other person's opinion. All you need to say is "thank you". That's it. You don't have to agree with the compliment.

Open up and experience what it is like to let the positive feedback in. Be aware of your negative self-talk while you are doing so. Your self-talk can be quite informative and can help you become aware of what is blocking you from accepting compliments.

Avoid playing the victim

The same applies to you when you attempt to blame others for the problems in your relationship. When clients tell me about their relationship they often focus on everything the other person has done wrong and said wrong. For example, one woman told me that her partner is always worried about money and how he tells her that they both have to work harder and save more. She says she takes each of these comments personally and feels like he is blaming her. She tells me this in a voice tone that indicates that she thinks he is wrong and expects me to agree with her.

It is important in these situations to remember that the other person has the right to think and want what they want. He has the right to feel what he feels even if it causes some difficulties for her and may be uncomfortable for her.

Her reaction to his comments is her choice and not his fault. Just as he has the right to think and feel the way he does, she is responsible for her reaction, her feelings and thoughts. He may keep his pattern of behaviour going, but I ask her *"what are you willing to do differently about the situation?"* It is up to her to set her boundaries and to say what she wants or needs. She can't change him but she can change her reaction to him and she can communicate her perspective on the situation to him.

That is not about me.

When we are in a new relationship we often bring baggage to that relationship in the form of people from the past. We react to the current person as if he/she were our ex-wife, ex-boss, brother or mother. When you recognize this is happening in your relationship it is up to you to remind the other person, "That is not about me. I am not…" and then keep the discussion focused on your current relationship.

And at the same time, if you find yourself reacting to someone as if they were someone else from your past, you need to remind yourself that your reaction is not about this current person. For example, telling yourself, "He is not Michael. There is nothing Bill has done for me to feel this way toward him."

Don't try to argue someone out of his/her opinion.

When you try to convince someone that his/her opinion is wrong, a power struggle will often erupt. The underlining message is that there is only one reality and that is mine; that we all must think alike; that you must think the same way I do in order for me to feel safe in my opinion.

However, there are as many realities as there are people in the world. By trying to convince someone that how he thinks is wrong, you are not respecting his opinion. Just as you would like him to respect you, it is important for you to respect him.

Next time you are in a power struggle with someone ask yourself. *"Why?" "What am I hoping to achieve?" "Why do I need him to think the same way I do?"*

Avoid trying to be a mind-reader

When someone keeps hinting at their anger or their feelings, but does not come right out and express them, you don't have try to read their mind. You don't have to guess at what they are really wanting to say, but aren't. This is a form of "game playing".

Instead, take them at face value. Leave it up to them to tell you. Don't try to read their mind. If they choose not to tell you and expect you to read their mind that is their choice. But you don't have to do it. You do not have to rush in and try to fix it or interpret what they are feeling.

This can be a form of manipulation and passive-aggression. Allow them the opportunity to develop the courage to speak up for themselves. You don't have to work extra hard simply because they are not willing to take the risk.

For example, D. was dreading her meeting with a friend because she was sure that her friend was going to be angry that she said "no" to her the previous week. D. was willing to talk to her, but figured that her friend would not bring the topic up although she was likely to be mad. I asked D. if she wanted to bring it up and she said "no" because it wasn't an issue for her anymore. But she figured her friend would expect her to bring it up. If it was truly not an issue for D. anymore, I suggested that she not initiate the topic and leave it up to her friend to take responsibility to initiate the conversation. Even if the friend appears to be non-verbally trying to force D. to bring it up, she doesn't have to do so.

Dealing with criticism

When someone else criticizes you it tells you nothing about you. It only tells you the other person's opinion. By taking the criticism personally we are assuming that the other person is right and we are wrong. Why is that?

We can say to them, "Perhaps that is true. I will consider it". This doesn't mean that you have to do anything about it. The other person will often back off because all they want is to be acknowledged.

Responding assertively to criticism from others

1. Allow yourself to listen carefully to what the other person is saying. Remember it is just their opinion and they have the right to have their opinion.

2. Paraphrase the criticism so that the person knows you really "heard" and understood their point.

3. Decide whether the criticism is fair or unfair. Yes, sometimes the other person may have made a very good point, but simply expressed it in an ineffective way.

4. Ask the critic for more detail if they appear to be hinting or being vague. This requires them to think through the feedback more thoroughly and be more concrete and specific.

5. If it's fair criticism, ask for specific suggestions or alternatives, such as what you might do to handle the situation or behave differently. "Yes, my garden is a mess. What do you think is the first thing I need to do?"

6. Avoid beating up on yourself and making excuses.

7. If you disagree with the criticism, respond with "I" statements rather than "You" statements.

8. Simply agreeing with the critic stops criticism immediately since your refusal to argue has made further talk unnecessary. Say, "You're right, I could have arrived on time if I had tried harder."

9. Use the "perhaps" technique discussed below or "it's possible you're right" even if the chances are very minimal.

Perhaps...

When someone criticizes you or gives you unsolicited advice one word that is helpful when responding to them is "perhaps". For example, "perhaps I could have phoned first", "perhaps, I could have done a better job on that report", "perhaps, I did need that job".

"Perhaps" acknowledges what the other person has said, but does not imply agreement with them. You have not agreed to do what they suggested; you are simply indicating that it is a possibility or an option. When someone offers their opinion or feedback to you, they usually only want to know that you have heard what they said. By saying perhaps and repeating back what they have said, they know that you have heard them. If you simply try to ignore them, they will often get louder and more persistent thinking that you have not heard. Then when they ask you, "well are you going to do it", you can simply once again respond with, "perhaps". ☺

Avoid keeping score

When someone criticizes us our tendency often is to defend ourselves in order to feel safe. One way we do this is by keeping score. By this I mean that when you tell me what I've done wrong, I have to tell you what you've also done wrong. This leads you to defending yourself by pointing out how I have failed and then I have to do the same. Each of us tries to out maneuver the other person either by listing what <u>we</u> have done right or what <u>they</u> have done wrong.

This simply creates a power struggle and the only way out of a power struggle is for one person to stop. It takes two people to play a game and keep it going. When someone is critical don't be critical back in order for you to feel stronger. By doing this you are simply repeating and perpetuating their behaviour.

Instead, be assertive and let them know that what they have said to you is not appropriate. Let them know how you feel. Avoid attacking them back which will only perpetuate a power struggle. You don't need to defend yourself.

A technique to use in this situation is to simply reflect back or acknowledge the other person's opinion. For example, "So you are really frustrated that I still haven't made a decision about changing my job". And then just leave it at that. No need to agree or disagree with what they said. They have the right to have their opinion and you have the right to have yours. Both opinions can exist at the same time. Usually the other person just wants to know that you heard them and by acknowledging what they have said and paraphrasing it back to them you let them know that you heard them, and heard them correctly.

You will likely feel most inclined to defend yourself when there is a part of you that agrees with what the other person has said. When this occurs their comment ends up pressing your buttons and while defending yourself to them, you are at the same time justifying your behaviour to yourself.

The blame game

Similar to the discussion above about power struggles, the same applies when someone blames you for something. Simply reflect back to them their opinion that they think you are responsible for the situation. Avoid wasting your energy arguing with them or justifying your behaviour. Just because they believe something does not automatically make it so. Remember it is only their opinion or perception of the situation and it is okay for you to agree to disagree.

That's not my problem

When you are assertive with others and ask for what you want or say no to a request, often the other person will start coming up with all the reasons why you have to say yes or all the reasons why they can't meet your request. They usually focus on the difficulties that it will create for them.

One way to respond to their justifications or complaints is to say, "that is not my problem". For example, when I ask my landlord to repair my furnace and he hesitates and says how much money he's just had to spend on one of the other units and how busy he is, my response could be "I hear that right now is not a convenient time for you and you have had a lot of other expenses and that's not my problem, I still want you to fix my furnace."

Blah, blah, blah. Now back to what we were talking about

When we start to be assertive, others may respond by trying to distract us from our focus. This distraction can come in many forms. Think of it as two people leaving on a journey supposedly with the same destination in mind when actually they are heading for two very different places. For example when a parent asks a teenager to clean up their bedroom…

See the Figure 3 on the following page. The parent starts off asking the teenager to clean his room (1). In order to avoid doing this the teenager distracts his mom by yelling, complaining and comparing her to his friend's mom (2). What usually happens now is that the mom gets triggered and goes rushing over to the son's side. "Don't talk to me like that!" (3)

Who is now in charge of the conversation? The son! He has taken his mom directly off topic in order to get his way.

We all have ways that we distract others when we don't want to discuss a topic. For example, I had a friend who distracted me by saying "I guess I can't do anything right" ☹ Initially I wanted to avoid conflict, so of course I went right over to his side and said "no, no, no I don't mean that, there's nothing wrong with you". When I caught on to what I was allowing to happen. I changed my response to "I'm not going there. You can go there if you like. When you are finished I still want to talk about the…" I did not allow myself to be sucked in to his distraction. "Blah, Blah, blah, now back to what we were talking about."

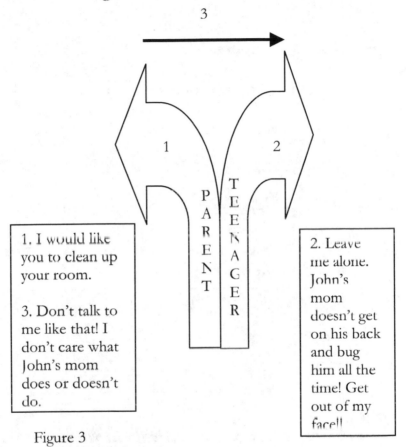

1. I would like you to clean up your room.

3. Don't talk to me like that! I don't care what John's mom does or doesn't do.

2. Leave me alone. John's mom doesn't get on his back and bug him all the time! Get out of my face!!

Figure 3

How do you distract others when you don't want to talk about something? For example, I tend to start telling the other person what to do, give advice, and try to control them, which are all effective ways to get the attention off of me!

If you could do it differently...

Think of a time when you were not assertive. Write out in detail a complete description of that situation. Include:

- *When it happened*

- *Who was involved in the interaction*

- *Where it took place*

- *What happened*

- *How you responded in the situation*

- *Why were you not assertive the first time? What got in the way?*

- *By not being assertive, which of your goals did not get met?*

Now is your chance to respond to the situation differently.

If you were to respond assertively in this situation, what would you have said and done differently?

Try this exercise with several situations. Eventually assertive responses will become more familiar and you will respond assertively at the time of the interaction rather than looking back afterwards. Good luck!

7

What Do I Need to Remember?

1. Begin being assertive in low risk situations first.

2. Practice makes perfect. Don't expect immediate success in expressing yourself assertively.

3. Acknowledge your successes. Remember the feelings associated with a positive outcome.

4. Don't expect to always get what you want. Satisfaction comes from validating yourself through expressing yourself.

5. Others will not always like your assertive behaviour. It doesn't mean that you do not have the right to be assertive.

6. Learn from your mistakes.

7. You don't have to be an expert to offer an opinion.

8. Don't expect to be guilt-free every time you are assertive. You can feel guilty and be assertive at the same time.

9. Assess each situation and respond appropriately.

10. If someone interrupts you when you are speaking, ask that person to wait until you have finished your statement. For example, "please wait a minute and let me finish speaking."

11. Ensure your body language is also assertive. Assertive body language includes the following:
    - maintaining direct eye contact
    - speaking clearly
    - using appropriate voice tone
    - respecting personal space
    - using open body language

12. Thinking positively about being assertive makes it easier to actually be assertive.

13. Make sure your responses are clear and concise.

14. You have the right to be assertive and express your feelings, wants and opinions.

About the author:

Barbara Small has a Bachelor's degree in Psychology and a Master's degree in Counselling. She is also trained as a Life Coach. She has been working with clients in private practice for over a decade. Barb facilitates workshops on various topics; including assertiveness skills, group facilitation skills, positive self-talk and communication skills. She also teaches Counselling Support Skills at the local college. Barb lives and works in Victoria, BC.

Additional copies of this book can be purchased from the author. Contact Barb at:
Tel: (250) 384-9020
Fax: (250) 384-9024
Email: barbsmall@shaw.ca
www.barbsmallcounselling-coaching.com

Look for Barb's next book coming out in early 2006: *"Blah, Blah, Blah: Stopping That Negative Self-talk"*

ISBN 141206931-9